WATER FROM
MY WELL

*Finding God In
The Midst Of Life,
Love And Loneliness*

ERIC ELDER

ISBN 978-1-931760-81-2

DEDICATION

To my dear friends who
encourage me to go deeper.

TABLE OF CONTENTS

Introduction

WATER FROM MY WELL

One of my favorite books to read when I was first venturing into the world on my own was a collection of essays by E.B. White called simply *Essays of E.B. White.*

White was famous for writing not only children's books like *Charlotte's Web* and *Stuart Little,* but also for writing an elegant grammar book which I—and many others—used in English classes over the years called *The Elements of Style.*

I loved White's essays in particular, not only because they were written so fluidly, but because they gave me a glimpse into his heart and soul. I could see the scenes he was describing. I could feel the feelings he felt. He put words to my thoughts which I was only beginning to formulate in my mind, like this one from an essay called "Years of Wonder":

"I wanted to test myself—throw myself into any flame that was handy, to see if I could stand the heat."

Like E.B. White, I've written the messages in this book as a way to give you a glimpse into my own heart and soul. Maybe you'll relate to some of the things I've shared here, whether it's the excitement and difficulty of setting and keeping goals, or what to do when you run up against boulders in the rivers of your life. These messages were written over a period of several months in 2016, a year that for me was filled with a combination of life, love and loneliness. Yet through it all, I was thankful to know that God was right there with me, every step of the way. I pray these messages will bring life and refreshment to your soul like water from a well—in this case, water drawn from my own personal well.

Read. Explore. Enjoy!

And thanks for coming along with me on my journey! As you'll see in Chapter 20, this is just the beginning—the best is yet to come!

Eric Elder

1

IT'S THAT
TIME OF YEAR

I was listening to a song on the radio one day with my 21-year-old daughter, Makari, and I said to her, "I wish I could write a song like that."

She turned to me and said, "You can!"

"Really?!?" I said. "Do you think so?"

"Of course, you can!" she replied, with total confidence in my abilities.

As I sat there and thought about her statement, I couldn't believe how much her simple belief in me changed my whole attitude towards the idea of writing a song that other people might come to love as much as I loved listening to that song on the radio.

Although I had written songs before, ever since having that conversation with my daughter I've written several songs that I've come to love as much as the song I heard on the radio that day! I haven't published them yet, but I hope to do so someday. And perhaps someday, someone else will be blessed by my music as much as I've been blessed by the music of others.

I tell you that story to encourage you to set some goals for yourself that you can *believe in*. What a difference it makes to have even *one* confidence-boosting statement come into your mind, one statement that will help you reach for and attain that which God has put on your heart to do and enabled you to do.

My good friend, Kent Sanders, has encouraged me in my own goal-setting this year in a book he wrote called *The Artist's Suitcase*. In his chapter called "Y is for Year," Kent gave me a great idea for envisioning myself at the end of the year, trying to imagine myself doing some things that I'm not doing now.

One of the things I envisioned was a picture of myself, holding onto a finished script and score for a new musical I'm working on based on the life of St. Nicholas, a book which my wife and I wrote as a novella a few years ago. I had already begun writing the first three scenes and songs for the musical at the end of last year, and with my new Kent-inspired vision in mind, I could actually see myself finishing the whole thing by the end of this year—holding a copy of the completed script and score in my hand!

I'm telling you this now, that this is one of my goals, as an extra incentive to help me stick to that plan! I'm also planning to chat with Kent and another good friend by phone for an hour each week to help us all keep on track with the visions God has put on each of our hearts. I can't tell you how much it helped me last year to do this as Kent and I both had books we wanted to write. By talking to each other each week about our progress, and reading each other's work as we went along, we both launched our books last year on the same day. Even though our books were on different topics, our mutual goal of writing and publishing a book kept us on track all year long.

I'm telling you this not only for my own accountability, but to encourage you in your own goal setting. What are some things God has put on your heart for the coming year? What would you like to change, improve, or see differently in your life, if you could envision or change one or two (or ten or fifteen) things by the end of the year?

Regardless of how you fared on last year's

goals, today is a new day! This year is a new year. Perhaps part of your answer to achieving your goals in the coming year is contained in the things I've shared with you here:

1) Go ahead and dream. Envision yourself one year from now and what you would hope would be different in your life. This is not a pipe dream. This is an essential dream to help you move forward. As the Bible says: *"Where there is no vision, the people perish" (Proverbs 29:18, KJV).*

2) Believe you can do it. This doesn't have to be just positive "self talk." Run your ideas past God and others. Let them speak into your life to help give you the confidence you need or the clarity to sharpen your idea, like I received from my daughter when I told her about my desire to write a song that really moved people. If God has put a desire on your heart, trust Him to help you carry it out to completion. As Paul said to the Philippians: *"I thank my God every time I remember you... being confident of this, that He who began a good work in you will* *carry it on to completion until the day of Christ Jesus" (Philippians 1:1, 6, NIV).*

3) Enlist someone to walk with you towards achieving your goal. Whether you ask a friend, a mentor, a pastor, a small group leader, a cousin, a relative, your parents or your children, pick one, two or three others with whom you can talk about your goals and walk with you towards achieving them on a regular basis throughout the year. They'll be honored and you'll increase your chances of success exponentially. As King Solomon wrote: *"Two are better than one, because they have a good return for their work: If one falls down, his friend can help him up… A cord of three strands is not quickly broken" (Ecclesiastes 4:9, 10a, 12b, NIV).*

Go ahead and dream. Believe you can do it. Enlist someone to walk with you towards achieving your goals. I know you can do whatever God has put on your heart to do! If He's really put it there, He'll certainly help you to achieve it! As Paul said to the Ephesians:

"For we are God's workmanship, created in

Christ Jesus to do good works, which God pre-pared in advance for us to do" (Ephesians 2:10, *NIV*).

You can do it! I know you can!

2

WHEN CALLS
THE HEART

My daughter, Makari, and I met last weekend in Vancouver, British Columbia, to be on the set and meet the cast and crew of the Hallmark television series *When Calls The Heart.*

I'd like to share some stories and pictures with you from the weekend and encourage you to trust God with your whole heart. As I told some of the cast and crew, for me this isn't just a TV show; it's a weekly boost in my faith that heals, inspires and touches my heart in a deep, deep way.

And that's no accident.

Fourteen years ago, I had an occasion to interact with Brian Bird, one of the shows executive producers (along with Michael Landon, Jr). I had sent an email to Brian back when he was writing and producing another TV series called *Touched By An Angel. Touched* was one of the few TV shows we could watch together as a family, just like *When Calls The Heart* is now.

And that was no accident either.

Makari and I with actors Daniel Lissing ("Jack") and Erin Krakow ("Elizabeth"), Mamie Laverock ("Rosaleen") and Mitchell Kummen ("Gabe"), and Jesse Hutch ("Luke" on Debbie Macomber's Cedar Cove)

Brian Bird and those involved in the production of both of these shows wanted to create high quality, uplifting programming that inspired faith in the hearts of its viewers, rather than denigrating their faith. I wrote to Brian all those years ago because I wanted to express to him my sincere thanks for his work on *Touched*. It wasn't just a show to distract us from our lives; it was a show to help us live our lives better. Like going to church, *Touched* gave us a weekly boost in our faith—and the hope to keep going on—by giving us very real and very practical messages on topics ranging from death and forgiveness to building better relationships.

But to tell my story properly, I really have to back up to two weeks before I wrote that first email to Brian Bird fourteen years ago, as I had never even heard of him before. What was really on my heart was that I wanted to write a letter to Martha Williamson, the executive producer of *Touched By An Angel*. I had just finished reading a book she had written in which she told why she latched onto the show in the first place—and how she helped to shape it to be so faith-inspiring. I was so thankful for her tenacity to take on this project and stick to her convictions that I wanted to write her a letter of sincere thanks.

But I had never written to a television exec

before! How would I find her? How would I get a letter through to her? And what were the chances that she would ever see what I wrote at all, given the mounds of fan mail they must receive every day?

I didn't have time to write a heartfelt letter that no one would ever read. And more than likely, I thought, my letter would probably just end up as some statistic showing that one more viewer liked their show. I had much more to say than that, and it wasn't worth my time if my letter would just end up as a checkmark on some tally sheet for a busy senior executive.

I had literally 1,000 emails of my own that were awaiting replies in my own inbox, some of which had been waiting for months, and I decided to take care of that important correspondence first before I sat down to write to Martha Williamson. I told myself if I got my inbox down to zero, then I would write a letter to her.

To my surprise, two weeks later I had finished answering every email in my inbox, plus all the new ones that came in during those two weeks (plus the new ones that came as responses to my responses!) My inbox was showing that rare (and never-to-be-repeated) number of emails as "zero." Having achieved that miraculous goal, I knew it was time to write a letter to Martha Williamson.

So I did. I spent the rest of the day trying to think of how best to communicate my sincere thanks. By Friday afternoon, I had finished.

The next question was how to get the letter to her. But I was worn out and decided to wait until the following week to figure out that part of the puzzle.

On Saturday night, our family watched *Touched* once again, and once again we were moved to tears and greater faith by the story we saw.

On Sunday morning, I got an email from one of my subscribers on my mailing list who gets my weekly messages. He asked if I could change his email to a new address so he could keep getting my messages. My wife was looking over my shoulder as I was reading his email and noticed that his name was "Al Lowry."

"Al Lowry?" she said. "Wasn't that the name of the dad in last night's episode of *Touched By An Angel?*"

I remembered his name, too, because "LOWRY" had been written in bold letters on the back of his daughter's basketball jersey in one of the scenes.

"Yeah, I think it was," I said.

So I wrote to "Al Lowry" and told him that I changed his email address, adding that it was funny because he had the same name as a character on *Touched By An Angel* that we had seen the night before.

Al wrote back to say that it *was* funny because the guy who wrote that episode is in his small group at his church and had used Al's name as a character name in the show!

What?!?! I couldn't believe it! I did a quick search on the Internet to find the name of the writer, Brian Bird, and discovered that he was not only a writer, but also that he was a co-producer with Martha Williamson!

Here I had been praying about how to get a letter to Martha Williamson to thank her for the show, and I was reluctant to even write the letter because I thought she would never read it! But now I had a way that I might actually be able to get it into her hands!

I told Al what I had been trying to do and asked if he could pass along my letter to Brian. He said he would, and Brian himself wrote back to say he'd pass it along to Martha Williamson!

Brian also wrote to ask me if I could send my letter to the network also, as they were in the midst of trying to decide whether or not to renew the show for another season. Brian said that the network gave serious consideration to letters from viewers like mine, so he sent me the addresses where I could also send my letter. A few weeks later, I learned that the show *had* been renewed for one more season, and another twenty-some episodes.

Did my letter make any difference? I can't say for sure. But I do know that God had put it on my heart to write it, so I did my part. Then He did *His* part and put it in the hands of someone who could do something with it. Praise God! Whatever the reason it was renewed, my family and I were able to enjoy the show every week for another year—along with millions of others who were also touched by *Touched*.

In the years that followed, Al Lowry became a good personal friend of mine, eventually joining our ministry as a member of our board of directors. I continued to correspond with Brian, who was, and still is, a tremendous inspiration to me in my own writing, as we both continue to do our best to touch people with high quality, uplifting and faith-affirming messages.

Makari and I with executive producers Brian Bird and his wife Patty, Michael Landon, Jr., and director Neill Fearnley and writers Derek Thompson and Robin Bernheim.

Although I've kept in touch with Brian over the years by email, Facebook and phone, this weekend was the first time we met face-to-face! Brian had invited my daughter and me to a special event he had put together for a small group of fans and friends of *When Calls The Heart*, as Brian knew that my daughter is going into acting. It was a total blast.

In one sense, meeting Brian in person wasn't a big deal for we had been conversing for the past fourteen years. But in another sense, meeting him in person WAS a big deal as the seeds of our growing friendship—and the mutual encouragement that we've gained—had been planted so many years ago. That one small act of following through with what God had put on my heart has yielded numerous benefits not only for me and Brian and Al, but for all those who have been touched by the work we've *all* been able to do, both apart and together. Who knows what might happen from here?

As for me, I'm glad I trusted God and did what He put on my heart to do all those years ago and all along the way.

What about you? Is there something God is putting on your heart to do today? Listen to His call, give it a chance, then follow through. See what God might do with it! Trust Him from the bottom of your heart, do your part and let Him take care of the rest.

As the Bible says:

> *"Trust God from the bottom of your heart; don't try to figure out everything on your own. Listen for God's voice in everything you do, everywhere you go; He's the one who will keep you on track"* *(Proverbs 3:5-6, MSG).*

3

ASKING
FOR BLESSINGS

Last month I had the rare opportunity to meet Janette Oke, author of the book which served as the basis for the new television series running on the Hallmark Channel called *When Calls The Heart*. My daughter and I were invited to attend a special event on the set near Vancouver where the show is filmed, as my daughter is going into acting. I have to admit, I've never read any of Janette Oke's books before; I've only seen them all over the shelves in bookstores (she's written over 75 novels, selling more than 30 million books!)

And yet, when the key people were introduced at a gathering for fans and friends of the show on Friday night—including actors, producers and script writers—I was floored when Janette was introduced. Why? Because here was the woman behind this entire "world" I had been watching for two years on

TV with my family. She's the one who envisioned the characters, described the settings and infused them with her faith and values. While it's taken hundreds of cast and crew members to bring that world to the screen, it all started in her mind 33 years ago when she first wrote the book *When Calls The Heart* (she's now 81 years young).

As a writer myself, I was struck by how our words can have an effect on people all over the world, even decades or generations after our words are first written. I thought, *I would love to have a portion of whatever God has given to Janette!*

When I saw her at one point during the night standing in the ballroom with only one or two others around her, I thought perhaps I could ask her to pray for me. Although I didn't know what she might say, I thought it was worth it to try. I walked over and introduced myself, saying, "Thank you for using your gift to reach so many people, including me. I'm a writer, too, and I wondered if you would pray for me, that God would use my words to reach many people for His kingdom as well?"

Janette said she'd be glad to pray for me!

She pulled me in close and launched into a beautiful one or two minute prayer, speaking directly into my ear.

After praying, she signed a notebook I was carrying, writing, *"Eric, May God continue to lead you. Janette Oke."*

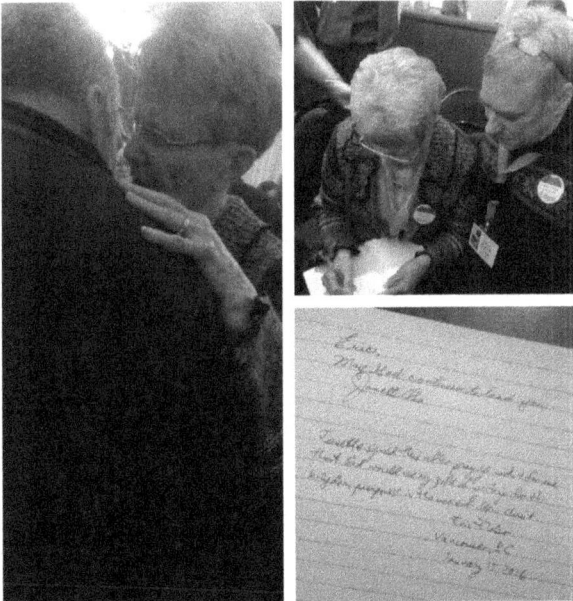

Janette Oke praying for me and signing my notepad the night before my daughter and I visited the set of When Calls The Heart, a Hallmark TV series based on Janette's book by the same title.

It may seem bold or unusual to ask someone to bless you with a portion of that which God has blessed them. Yet it's not the first time I've asked someone to pray for me like that. I've taken courage from those in the Bible who have asked others to bless them as well, like Elisha asking for a blessing from Elijah: *"Let me inherit a double portion of your spirit" (2 Kings 2:9b, NIV);* or Jacob asking for a blessing from the man with whom he had been wrestling all night: *"I will not let you go unless you bless me!" (Genesis 32:26b, NIV).*

It's not that I'm expecting instant answers from these prayers of blessing, and it's not like I'm trying to rub a magical charm for good luck. It's simply asking for a prayer of blessing from those whom God has already blessed. And as a believer in prayer, I trust that God will answer those prayers some day, in some way—and even in ways that might go beyond all I could ask or imagine.

I remember asking a famous singer one time if he would pray for my voice. He said, "Sure," then asked, "What happened to your voice?" thinking that perhaps I had injured it in some way.

I said, "Oh, my voice is fine, I just wish I

could sing like you!" He laughed, then prayed for me, gladly. It's not that I thought my voice would suddenly change to sound like his, for we're all gifted and wired in unique ways. He didn't get to where he was by just a prayer—it takes lots of hard work, training and "practice, practice, practice."

But I also know that Jesus has "good gifts" He wants to give us, and He encourages us to ask in order to receive them. As Jesus said:

> *"Ask and it will be given to you; seek and you will find; knock and the door will be opened to you. For everyone who asks receives; the one who seeks finds; and to the one who knocks, the door will be opened" (Matthew 7:7-8, NIV).*

My daughter and I asked for prayers of blessings from two other people during our weekend on the set.

We met the father of one of the child actors on the show and were able to talk with him about how their family got connected with the production. As he answered our questions, I thought, *Wouldn't it be great if he would pray for my daughter that God would open some similar doors for her?* I didn't even know if he was a Christian or not. But at one point while we were talking, he mentioned how "blessed" he felt by all that had happened to their family. I decided then and there that it was worth asking him for a blessing, too.

I asked, "Would you mind praying for my daughter that God would bless her as you and your family have been blessed?"

He paused for a moment, then said, "No one has ever asked me to do that before. But sure, I'd be glad to." He took our hands in his and prayed an honest, godly and heart warming prayer.

The third prayer of blessing we received came at the end of the weekend's activities when my daughter talked to an actor with whom she was very impressed. He wasn't an actor on this particular show, but happened to be on the set that day with us. Again, we weren't sure if he was a Christian or not, but we had heard from a member of the crew that they thought he was involved with a church nearby. My daughter stepped up to talk to him, looked at him sincerely and asked, "Would you pray for me? I'm going into acting, too, and I would love to receive what you have."

He looked at her and said, "Not many people ask me that! But okay, let's pray." He then launched into a lengthy prayer for her, which turned into a 45-minute conversation about acting, Hollywood, boundaries and balancing work and family life. That prayer and conversation turned out to be the highlight of the whole weekend for my daughter.

I tell you these stories not to be a name dropper, for I have no interest in that. I tell you these stories because I want to encourage YOU to ask for blessings from those you meet—those who have been gifted in ways that you may want to grow, too.

It's good to check your motives before asking for a blessing, as this isn't meant to be a substitute to try to curry someone's favor or as a way to get close enough to someone to get their autograph! It's simply and truly a way to ask God to bless you as others have been blessed. If that's your desire, then let me encourage you to consider asking, too! If the person you ask says, "Yes," then receive whatever blessing God chooses to pour out on you. Who knows how your life and the lives of those around you—perhaps even the lives of people all around the world for generations to come—might be affected by your asking!

When I came home from our weekend in Vancouver, a friend told me that she had been praying that I would receive everything God wanted me to receive on the trip. As I thought about her prayers, I thought about those three blessings that others had prayed over my daughter and me. I thought, *Yes, Lord, I think I have received everything You wanted me to receive.*

Ask and it will be given to you; seek and you will find; knock and the door will be opened to you. Ask God, yes, but don't be afraid to ask people sometimes, too. Their prayers of blessings may rock more than just your world.

4

FINDING
GOD'S PROVISION

Are you in need of something from God today? If so, let me encourage you (as a friend recently encouraged me) that "God's provision is there before the need has presented itself. It is merely a matter of the light shining on the provision so it can be seen."

I've been amazed to see this truth lived out in my own life over the last few weeks.

A few weeks ago, I was talking to another friend who shared with me, rather unintentionally, that his family was down to their last $49 in their bank account. He was trying hard to fill it back up, but his hard work wasn't bearing as much fruit as he needed.

He had done so much for me over the years that I wondered what I could do for him. I looked in my own bank account and saw that I had $500.36. Before I had time to talk myself out of it, I wrote out a check for

$500 and put it in the mail to my friend. I knew it was the right thing to do. I just had to trust that God would somehow provide for us both.

The day my check arrived at my friend's house, another need presented itself—this time, a bill I hadn't anticipated for $2,000! To make matters worse, I got a message from my bank saying that a check I had deposited a few months earlier had accidentally been deposited twice, so they were removing the amount of that check—which happened to be $500—from my bank account! I then found out from my friend that same day that my check to him for $500 had just arrived at his house!

I took a deep breath and said, "God, I know You were prompting me to do this. I'm going to have to trust You to cover it." I was headed out of town for the weekend, and I didn't have time to think about it or to hardly even worry about. I had to trust God that He would work it out.

When I got back from my trip, I saw an email in my inbox that I had already seen just before I left for my trip, but I had simply ignored it because it looked like spam. It was from an agent for a company who said he had a client who was interested in buying one of the domain names I owned (a domain name is a website address, like www.theranch.org or www.thisdaysthought.org; I've bought and used several domain names over the years for different projects, each of which has cost me about $15 a year.)

I checked out this agent's website, and the company did look legitimate. The domain name their client wanted to buy was one which I had used many years ago—and thought I might use again some day—but I wasn't sure if I ever would. So I wrote to the agent and asked what his client was offering to pay for the domain name.

He wrote back and said, "$1,000."

$1,000! I couldn't believe it! On one hand, I wanted to jump at the opportunity. But on the other hand, I was still wondering if maybe I should hang onto that domain name in case I decided to use it again someday.

I thought, *If they had offered me $10,000, that would be a no-brainer. I'd just pick out another domain name if I ever needed one in the future. But for $1,000, I'm not sure if I should give it up.*

There was a button on the agent's website where I could make a counter offer. I thought about entering $10,000, but that seemed ridiculous. I would have been happy to have maybe $2,000-3,000 for it. But to have $10,000, that would certainly be an easy decision.

Not wanting to give it much more thought, especially since I still wondered if this was even a legitimate offer, I clicked the button to make a counter offer, I entered $10,000 and then I pushed "Send."

A few hours later, I got an email saying that the client was willing to offer $2,500, but that would be their final offer.

$2,500! That was right in between the $2,000-3,000 that I said I would be happy with! And not coincidentally, that was exactly the amount I was needing to cover my two unexpected expenses: $500 for my friend and $2,000 for myself.

"God, I can't believe it! I'm sorry I had so little faith!" Trusting now that it was God's provision, I clicked the button that said, "Accept Offer." By the end of the week, I had transferred my domain name to the client and had deposited their check into my bank account. My friend cashed the check I sent him, and I paid my unexpected bill.

When I looked back at the original email from the agent, I saw that it had come on the same morning that my friend had received my check (and I received the notice from my bank that it was $500 short), and the same day I received that unexpected bill for $2,000. God's provision was *already there* in my inbox. It was merely a matter of the light shining on the provision so it could be seen.

This reminded me of the unusual way Jesus paid a bill for a friend and Himself one day, too.

When a tax collector came to Jesus and Peter, asking them to pay their two-drachma "temple tax," Jesus gave Peter these unusual instructions. Jesus said:

> *"...go to the lake and throw out your line. Take the first fish you catch; open its mouth and you will find a four-drachma coin. Take it and give it to them for My tax and yours" (Matthew 17:27b, NIV).*

I can imagine the surprise on Peter's face when he threw out his fishing line, reeled in a fish and there in its mouth was a four-drachma coin!

The provision for both Peter and Jesus was there all along, either already in the fish's mouth, or perhaps on the bottom of the lake, just waiting for the God of the universe to direct the fish to nibble along until it picked up the coin in its mouth and went to the spot where Peter would be fishing. God's provision was *already there* before the need presented itself. It was merely a matter of the light shining on the provision so it could be seen.

I was thinking about sharing this story with you today, about God's provision for me, but then something else popped that made me hesitate. Yet another need had presented itself that I had no way of meeting. I thought, *God, how can I write this story about You providing for our needs even before the needs present themselves when I'm facing another need right now that I have no idea how I'm going to meet?!?* But then something amazing happened—just yesterday.

Back on Thursday, when this need arose, we had a terrible snowstorm. Schools and businesses were closed for the first time all winter. My mail had been delivered to my mailbox before the storm got too bad, but by the time I went out to the mailbox later in the day, the door to the mailbox had blown open by the storm. A magazine was hanging half-way out, soaked in snow. I wondered if anything else had blown out, and as I looked around, I did find a piece of junk mail almost completely covered by snow and soaking wet. I tried to look for any other mail that might have blown out, but the storm was too fierce to keep searching any further.

Then yesterday, when almost all of the snow had finally melted, I looked out in my yard. There were six pieces of mail strewn all over the yard that had been covered completely by snow just a few days before. I picked up each one, seeing that some were important and others were not—and one from a church where I used to attend. When I opened the last letter from the church, I was in shock! Enclosed was a check for the exact amount of the need I had learned about on the day of the snowstorm! A letter was attached explaining that the church wanted to give our ministry a special one-time gift from their surplus offerings from the previous year. This check was a portion of that surplus for the year! (In all the years since we attended that church, we had never received such a gift before. This was completely unexpected!)

Again, I was astounded, not only that the need was covered fully, but that it had been already covered on the very same day that the need had presented itself. God's provision *was* already there; it was merely hidden under a blanket of snow until the light of the sun shown upon it!

5

WHAT ARE YOU LOOKING FOR?

I've just returned from Israel, where I took my two youngest kids to celebrate Easter in the Holy Land. It was a terrific trip, the highlights of which were baptizing my kids in the Jordan River and worshipping with them the next day at the Garden Tomb in Jerusalem with other believers from all over the world. It was phenomenal!

I mean, how could it *not* be phenomenal? To be in the Holy Land on Easter morning, worshipping in a beautiful garden while looking at an empty tomb that dates back to the time of Christ. And then to be listening to Scriptures being read about what happened on that first Easter morning—events that took place right there in the city where I was worshipping?!?

Yet not everyone was so inspired. On our way out of the service, I heard a woman say (scream, really), "What a waste!"

She then continued her tirade as she walked down the street, cutting down everything that happened in that early morning worship service. She was fuming. Absolutely fuming.

I thought, *Were we even at the same service?* How could she *not* have been totally moved by the music, the message and all that happened during that sweet time in the presence of God?

I've seen the same thing happen at other sites throughout Israel. I remember the first time I ever stepped foot in the Church of the Holy Sepulcher, a church which had been built in the 4th century over the spot where believers had been shown for centuries where Christ was crucified. When I walked into the building, I fell to my knees and cried for at least ten minutes straight. I was so thankful for what Jesus had done for me there on that hill. It didn't matter to me that the church was filled with noise and people and an eclectic collection of artifacts that had been donated by kings and queens over two millennia. All I could see was the image of my Savior, saving me from my sins, as He died there on that hill nearly 2,000 years ago.

Yet as I walked out of *that* church, I heard people debating whether the church was beautiful or gaudy, whether this *was* or *was not* the true location of the crucifixion or if it was instead at the Garden Tomb a short walk away. Other people were shaking their heads at the chaos they had experienced inside, while still others were absolutely enthralled to have visited a place where their parents, and their grandparents before them, had made similar pilgrimages over the years.

While we were all looking at the same things, we were not all looking *for* the same things. And therein lied the difference: what we were looking *for* versus what we were looking *at*.

I shared this difference later in the week with our tour group of 38 people—because after five or six days of touring around, it could have been easy to start thinking that all we were seeing was a bunch of rocks. At the Church of the Holy Sepulcher, you can reach through a hole in the floor and touch the top of the rock that makes up the hill where Jesus died and over which the church was built. At the Garden Tomb, you can walk inside an empty tomb from the time of Christ, carved out of the rock in the hillside. In Bethlehem, you can walk down some stairs below the altar and touch a similar rock in a hole in the floor that marks where Jesus was likely born.

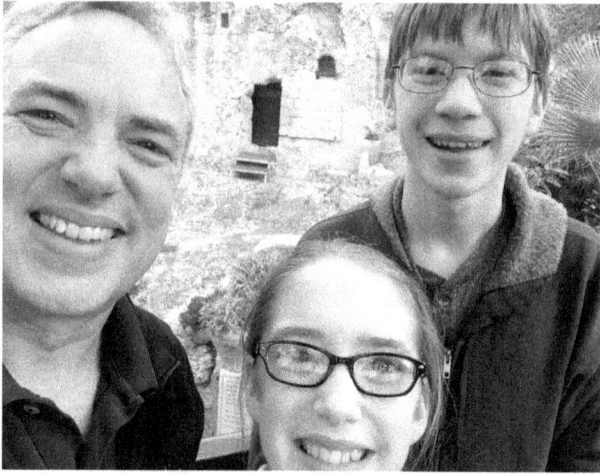

Bo, Kaleo and I at the Garden Tomb for Easter in Jerusalem.

Everywhere we went we saw *rocks*, whether it was the Western Wall (built out of rocks), or the Church of All Nations (built over the rock where Jesus wept in the Garden of Gethsemane), or the Temple Mount, on which stands the iconic "Dome of the Rock"—inside of which is… well, as the name clearly states… a rock!

And yet our trip was about *so much more* than rocks. It wasn't what we were looking *at* that was so important, but what we were looking *for*.

As I walked into the city of Capernaum, for instance, which contains broken columns of pillars from the ancient synagogue in that city, I was struck by the fact that Jesus healed and transformed the lives of two blind men there in that city when they put their faith in Him. That story was the same story that I was reading in my Bible—2,000 years later and 7,000 miles away—which inspired me to put my faith in Jesus. I felt I had been healed just as miraculously as those who had come to Jesus in Capernaum. And on this trip, I had in my backpack a copy of a book I had written in which I describe how Jesus changed my life when I read that story that took place in Capernaum.

I pulled out the book and showed it to our group, sharing with them what had happened to me 29 years ago when I read that story of what happened in Capernaum nearly 2,000 years later and 7,000 miles away. Yes, we were all looking at the ancient rocks of Capernaum, chiseled into the shapes of pillars and seats for a synagogue to use thousands of years ago. But it wasn't the rocks that I was thinking about as I testified to the group about what Jesus had done in my life. It was the Man who had walked among those rocks, the Man who had taught and healed and touched people's lives all those years ago and the Man who was still touching people's lives—like mine—all these years later.

Aside from the truth that we *were* looking at rocks, the bigger truth was that each of those rocks told a story. In fact, Jesus Himself said, when His followers were praising Him as He entered Jerusalem and the religious leaders told Him to silence His followers:

"I tell you, if they keep quiet, the stones will cry out" (Luke 19:40, NIV).

And here, 2,000 years later, those same stones *still* testify to the Savior who spoke those words!

As I shared my testimony with our group that day in Capernaum, I was thankful that it wasn't just the rocks which testified to the Savior. In the words of a terrific praise song from the 90's:

"I ain't gonna let no rock out-praise me!"

It was hard for me to walk around the Holy Land and think about much else *except* praise for my Savior who has touched me in so many ways. It wasn't what I was looking *at* that sparked such strong reactions within me, but what I was looking *for*.

What about you? What are you looking for today? Don't just focus on what you're looking at. Keep your eyes open wide. Who knows? God may even speak to you through a rock.

6

REMEMBERING
TO SMILE

Last weekend I had a chance to dance in a recital with my childhood dance teacher from 40 years ago. She's now teaching my daughter's tap class, and at the beginning of the school year, she said, "Eric, you don't have to sit out in the hallway. You can come and dance with us! Just take off your shoes and dance in your socks."

Part of me really wanted to do it. I loved my weekly tap classes as a kid. They always made me smile (and as my sister-in-law says, "How can you not smile when tapping?!").

But another part of me was really embarrassed by the idea. I'm over 50 (53 today, actually!) and I couldn't imagine how it would look to see myself in the classroom mirror, tapping again. But my tap teacher is now 75 and still tapping away. How could I say "No" to Miss Janet?

So I took off my shoes and went into the

classroom, along with my daughter and a few other moms and their daughters. By the end of the class I was hooked. I hadn't laughed so much or so long in a long, long time, and for that alone I told Miss Janet I'd be back again the following week. I went out and bought a pair of tap shoes and for the past 9 months have been tapping away with Miss Janet and my daughter every week.

Last weekend was the culmination of our year together, as I danced with my daughter and Miss Janet in her annual dance recital— her 60th since she began teaching—and she wanted to do it up right with a big bang.

She asked if I would dance with her in a special number at the end of the show, along with several other current and former students of hers. Again, I demurred, as I couldn't imagine dancing in a recital after all these years. But at 75, Miss Janet can still do the splits, so she wondered if I could dance with her and drop her down into the splits then pick her right back up again a couple times during the show.

She hooked me again. How could I say "No" to Miss Janet? So we did it! And we had a blast, laughing all the way.

Dancing with the Stars: my daughter and I rehearsing for one last dance with Miss Janet.

After the show, I gave Miss Janet a card and a picture, thanking her for the laughs and smiles. The picture I gave her was of a pewter statue my mom had given me back when I

was in high school, as my mom said it reminded her of me when I was a boy, taking acro-
bats from Miss Janet. The smile on the boy's
face was the same smile I had whenever I
walked on *my* hands. There was something
about it, walking on my hands and doing back
flips—just like tapping—that always made me
smile.

*A pewter statue my mom had given me years ago of a
boy doing what he loves.*

I told Miss Janet that I have put this statue on my desk from time to time over the years to remind myself to smile whenever I'm doing the work God has called me to do. Sometimes I get so bogged down in the details of the work that I forget to smile. I forget that *this* is what I was made for, *this* is what God has called me to do, created me to do and what I truly enjoy doing!

Whenever I look at this statue, it reminds me to smile. Not just when the work is done, not just when I'm on stage, not just when someone wants to take a picture, but right there in the midst of life, all along the way.

I love the quote of Eric Liddle, the Olympic runner who had a heart for missions. Although he wanted to move overseas to be a missionary, he also wanted to train for and run in the Olympics. When describing to a friend why he decided to run in the Olympics and wait until a later time o be a missionary, Eric said:

"When God created me, He made me fast. And when I run, I feel His pleasure."

There are some things in life that just bring

a smile to God's face—oftentimes the same things that bring smiles to our faces. And He loves bringing smiles to our faces. He loves bringing us joy. He loves bringing us laughter. He loves delighting us with the intimacies and ecstasies of life.

But with all the pressures, obstacles and heartaches that we face, it's sometimes easy to forget. We forget to smile.

It's not that life isn't hard. It's not that there aren't times when it's right to be sad. It's not that God wants us to fake it. But sometimes we just have to remind ourselves to smile. And when we do, it can open the door to bringing joy back to our lives. As the Bible says:

> *"A happy heart makes the face cheerful… the cheerful heart has a continual feast" (Proverbs 15: 13a, 15b).*

I was sad a few weeks ago when Miss Janet told me this would be her last recital and the end of her teaching career. After 60 years of teaching over 7,500 students, she was going to retire after the show. I wanted to cry. But looking at Miss Janet, how could I be sad? She had brought such joy back into my life. I had had so much fun all year that I was ready to take her class over and over again.

But as I told her in my card, I was so thankful she had invited me to dance with her for one more year, so thankful to dance with her in the recital and so thankful for the laughs and smiles again. I really needed them.

And whenever I was dancing with her, I didn't need the reminder.

Thank you, Miss Janet, and many blessings on your years ahead!

7

MOMENT
BY MOMENT

I'd like to encourage you today to put your trust in God for just one moment. Whatever you're facing, whatever you're working through, whatever you're dealing with or wondering about, put your trust in Him for just one moment.

Trust Him that He can walk you through it. Trust Him that He will help you all along the way. Trust Him that He will never leave you or forsake you, that He will never leave you alone, that He is working things out behind the scenes in ways that You could never imagine.

I shared a story yesterday at my son Josiah's graduation ceremony about his commitment to working hard on the things he loves. My wife and I homeschooled all six of our kids, and this was our fourth to graduate from high school. I was speaking to a group of fellow homeschooling families in the area

who had gathered to celebrate twenty-two se-
niors who were graduating this year. I said:

*"We hit a pretty major bump in our homeschool-
ing road about four years ago when my wife was
diagnosed with cancer, and sadly she passed away
just nine months after her diagnosis. Since I work
from home, my wife wanted me to keep homeschooling the kids, as long as I felt it was doable
for me and working for them. There were plenty of
days when I wasn't sure if it was doable for me or
working for them, but we had had days like that
before, so we all kept at it. I felt like some things
were slipping through the cracks, though, like con-
tinuing their piano lessons. I had taught them for
years when they were younger, and we had hired
teachers for them at other times, but it had been a
while since any of my kids had played at all. I
kept telling myself I should get them back into the
piano because they were all really good at it, but I
hadn't been able to do it yet.*

*"One night I came home from an event and heard
Josiah playing an incredible piece on the piano. I
hadn't heard him play in a long time and had never heard that particular piece before. I was
stunned, and I asked him when he learned to play
it. He said, 'Every time you're gone, I've been*

*working on it. I was going to wait until I had fin-
ished the whole piece to play it for you.' I about
burst into tears. (And I also thought, 'I should
leave more often!') But it really spoke to my heart
that even when I feel the weakest in my abilities, I
can trust my kids to God and His abilities, because He's able to do way more for them than I
could ever do. I also learned that I can trust my
kids, that if there's something they really want to
learn, they will."*

I had no idea that God, and my son, were
already working behind the scenes. As I
shared that story yesterday, I was reminded
that I could trust God for the things I'm facing today, and will face tomorrow, and the
next day, too.

I wrote a song for the piano about twenty
years ago called "Moment By Moment." I
wrote it after having attended a conference
where the topic one night was about the power of trusting in God—even for just one moment. The speaker asked us if we thought we
could put our trust in Him for just one moment, *that moment,* right then.

Yes, I thought, *I can certainly trust Him for a
moment.* She then asked if we could trust Him

again for the next moment, the one we were experiencing right then. Yes, of course, that was easy, too. I could trust Him for another moment.

She then said that if we could just keep trusting God like that, moment by moment, those moments would add up to minutes, minutes would add up to hours, and hours would add up to days, then months, then years. If we could keep trusting God moment by moment, we would end up trusting Him for the rest of our lives. "Don't underestimate what God can do in a moment," she said.

I had to agree. There's power in trusting God, even if it's just for one moment.

When I wrote the song "Moment By Moment" almost twenty years ago, I was just getting started with writing music. Although I loved playing the piano and had played my whole life, I had never written anything on my own until a friend walked up to me one day while I was practicing the piano. He gently closed the piano book in front of me and said, "Play now. I'd like to hear what you'd play if you didn't have someone else's music in front of you."

I stared at the closed book. Then I stared

at my friend. I stared back at the closed book again. I had no idea what to play! I had never played a song without sheet music in front of me. I sat there for over an hour, looking at the closed book, looking at my hands on the keys and talking to my friend about why I didn't know how to do what he was asking me to do.

But because of my friend's gesture of closing the book in front of me, and his genuine interest to hear what I would play if I were to play what was written on my heart—not just on the page—I gave it a try.

Over the next few weeks, I began turning those heart songs into piano songs that others could listen to and enjoy. "Moment By Moment" was one of the songs that came out, as I was reflecting on the idea of what could happen if I were to really trust God, even in a moment like that.

Last weekend, I had a chance to play that song on stage at our church during a time of communion. As I played, I couldn't help but reflect back to the time when I first wrote that song almost twenty years ago and how much God had done in my life over those twenty years. I was now playing that music that was written on my heart and letting God use it to touch the hearts of several thousand people who had gathered to worship Him that morning. Praise God!

I had trusted Him moment by moment, and all of those moments had turned into minutes, then hours, then days and months and years.

Don't underestimate what God can do in a moment, as the speaker encouraged us to consider all those years ago.

Keep putting your trust in Him, moment by moment. And when you do, you—and many others around you—will be blessed.

The sheet music for my song Moment By Moment, from my album called Clear My Mind.

8

My
Sanctuary

I'd like to encourage you this week to find a place where you can spend some quiet time with God. Not necessarily just a quiet place, but a place where you can really sense God's presence, where you can talk with Him and He can talk with you, where you can get away from the craziness of the world and enjoy spending time with the God who created you, who loves you and who cares about the things going on in your life even more than you care about them.

Whether it's a physical sanctuary in a church or a prayer closet in your home or a hammock swaying in the breeze between two trees, I pray that You'll be able to find your own kind of sanctuary this week—a place of refuge, a place where you can truly enjoy being in the presence of God.

I remember walking into a church sanctuary one day in the middle of the week. I was all by myself, and I thought I'd just sit down and play the piano. As I was sitting there calmly by myself, I suddenly realized that I wasn't alone. God Himself was right there with me. That church sanctuary became instantly transformed into a literal "sanctuary," a holy place where the presence of God had come to rest.

Having God's presence show up like that was such a wonderful feeling that I started writing a song about it while I was there. I called it, "My Sanctuary." It went, in part, like this:

"All I want
All I need
Is to be with You
And to know You're near.

"All I want
All I need
Is to talk with You
And to know You'll hear.

"And I know
There's a place
I can go to feel Your presence

Oh, Lord, bring me there
Bring me home."

I continued to write and sing a new song to the Lord that day, a song that had welled up within my soul and had come out as an expression of thankfulness to Him for showing up and being with me in that place.

The sheet music for my song My Sanctuary, as found on my album called Soothe My Soul.

Earlier this year I had a chance to walk through the streets of Jerusalem and go down inside the tunnels along the western wall of the Temple Mount area. Inside these tunnels, there's a place you pass that is the closest you can get these days to the "holy of holies," the place in the Temple in the days of King Solomon where God said His presence would dwell. That spot in the tunnels is a fairly holy spot still today, and God's presence still seems to exude from it. People come from all over the world to stand and pray at that spot near the wall. It's a holy spot, for sure, knowing that you're standing in a place that has been revered and hallowed by so many people over such a long span of years.

Yet I've experienced similar "holy places" in various spots around the world—not because anything particular happened on those spots at some point in history, but because I felt God's presence in those places in powerful ways that can only be described as holy moments.

Holy spots like these abound. And if a holy spot is defined by a place where God's presence dwells, then such a spot could be anywhere at any time, all around the world.

A few years ago a woman stayed at our house for a few months to help us repair and restore it. She had come from overseas to help us out as we worked on it, and she said she felt God's presence there in a particular way as she stayed. On the day she left, we were walking around the house looking at various aspects of it when she came to a plaque in the front entrance of the house. On it was a picture of a house with the words: "Home is where the (HEART) is." (There was a picture of a heart where the word "HEART" would have appeared.)

Our guest took out a pencil and wrote on the heart just one word in very small but distinct capital letters: LORD. The plaque now read what she had experienced there: "Home is where the LORD is." I've often been reminded of that truth as I look at that plaque. Home is not just where the heart is, but home is anywhere the LORD is. And since there's nowhere in the world that the LORD isn't, then we can come into His presence and get that sense of "home" anywhere in the world. We just need to be willing to take the time to seek Him, invite Him in and then acknowledge His presence when He is there.

There's a joy that comes from being in God's presence. There's a sense of safety, of comfort, of protection that comes from spending time with Him. A "sanctuary" is just such a place. It's a safe haven, an oasis, a shelter, a retreat, a hideaway, a port in the storm. But more than those things, a sanctuary is a place where the presence of God dwells.

That's why I want to encourage you this week to find a place where you can spend some quiet time with Him—a place where you can really experience the presence of God. A place where you can talk with Him and He can talk with you. A place where you can get away from the craziness of the world and enjoy spending some time with the God who created you, who loves you and who cares about the things going on in your life even more than you care about them.

My prayer is that you'll be able to find such a place. And when you do, I pray you'll feel right at home.

Will you pray with me?

Father, thank You for being a shelter in the storm, a place of refuge, a strong tower in our times of trouble. Lord, we come to You this week, looking for Your presence and eagerly desiring to spend some time with You. Help us to find that place, wherever it may be, so that we can spend some time with You, soaking up all You have to convey to us, and letting us share with You all that's on our hearts, too. Bring us into that place, Lord, and help us to come into it over and over and over again in the days ahead. In Jesus' name, Amen.

KEEPING YOUR FEET FORWARD AND YOUR KNEES BENT

A friend recently asked me, "How do you feel when you come across a boulder that's in your way?"

How do I feel? I didn't understand the question.

Maybe my friend meant to say, "What do you *do* when you come across a boulder that's in your way?" Because I know the answer to that one. I usually try to talk to the boulder (if the boulder is in the form of a person) or to God (if the boulder is related to finances or health or a person to whom I can't talk for some reason). I usually try to explain why I need to keep going the way I'm going, asking them to help me keep going or to move out of the way so I can get through.

But my friend said, "No, that's not what

I'm asking. I'm asking, 'How do you *feel* when you come across a boulder?'"

Again, I didn't understand the question. "Can I just go around the boulder?" I asked.

"Sure, you can go around it if you want to," my friend said. "But that's not what I'm asking. I'm asking, 'How you feel when you come across one that's in your way?'"

How do I feel? "Well," I said, "I usually feel frustrated. Angry. Hurt. Of course, that's how I feel. Isn't that obvious? Isn't that the way everyone feels?"

My friend didn't answer, but simply said, "I think there's something God wants to say to you. That's why I'm asking."

So over the next few days, I began to pray about the question: "How do I *feel* when I come across a boulder that's in my way?" The answer seemed so obvious that I didn't understand why it would even matter.

But while praying one day, I suddenly remembered something from many years ago—when I was just a kid. I was white-water rafting with my family on a river in Colorado. The guide who rented us the raft and was helping us to navigate the river gave us a helpful tip:

"If you fall out of the raft, float on your back with your feet forward and your knees bent. That way, if you run into a boulder underwater, you'll hit it with your feet first and be able to step up over it or push off and go around it. But if your feet aren't forward, you're likely to run into it with your back or your side or your head and you could get hurt pretty badly. And if your knees aren't bent, you won't be able to step up over it or push off and go around it. So be sure to keep your feet forward and your knees bent."

I've rafted and floated on many rivers since then, whether in the mountains of Nepal or on the plains here in Illinois, and I've always remembered that guide's advice. It's kept me from getting hurt several times.

So when I was praying about the boulder question, I remembered the guide's advice. And I suddenly realized that God *did* have something He wanted to say to me.

There have been times in my life when I've come across boulders that were in my way. Boulders that seemed to pop up out of nowhere. Boulders that threatened to derail me from the direction I was wanting to go.

And my reaction has almost always been the same. I get frustrated. Angry. Hurt.

I've tried talking to the boulders and talking to God. But when the boulders haven't moved, I've just gotten more frustrated. More angry. More hurt. Even when the boulders have moved, I've often felt the pain of running into the boulders long after I've moved on farther down the river.

White-water rafting in northern California with my son, Lucas, (middle-left) and my friend, Al Lowry (bottom-left). I'm on the top-left next to the guide. (June, 2005)

My friend's question made sense to me n o w. *What if,* I thought, *instead of getting sideswiped by the boulders that I come across in life, I change my posture, knowing that there are probably going to be more boulders ahead, and keep my feet forward and my knees bent so I can step up and over them or push off and go around them? It might not change the fact that I'll still run across some boulders —and it might still take some effort to get around them. But I might not get so frustrated when I come across them. I might not get so angry. I might not get so hurt.*

I began to think through some of the boulders I had run across in the past and how this advice could have helped me during those times: when I asked a boss for a favor, and he said no; when I asked a girl if she wanted to date, and she said no; when I asked God to change a situation, and He said no. In each situation, I remember getting frustrated. Angry. Hurt. I took their answers personally when oftentimes it wasn't personal at all, at least not at its core. In each situation, the others were just doing what they felt was right in the situation, but somehow it got personal from there.

As I thought about each of those situations from my past, I wondered, *What if I had kept my feet forward and my knees bent? How would I have reacted differently?* The biggest and most obvious difference was that I wouldn't have gotten nearly as frustrated, nearly as angry or nearly as hurt. I wouldn't have taken it all so personally. Instead, I could have stepped up and over the boulders, or pushed off and gone around them, rather than getting sideswiped, hit in the back, or knocked on the head.

I also thought about some of the boulders I'm facing now—those barriers that seem to be in my way and could potentially give me some real knocks, too, if I'm not prepared for them. I can easily see how I don't have to take it so personally if the boulders don't move. I can see it better from the boulders' perspectives. A boulder, after all, isn't necessarily at fault for being plopped down in the middle of the river. It's just sitting there innocently, perhaps, but happens to be in my way!

And while I know very well that my guide's advice can't prevent me from ever experiencing frustration or anger or hurt, it does give me a way to *minimize* or *eliminate* much of the frustration or anger or hurt. The big difference is posture. Preparedness. And not letting every obstacle seem so dang *personal*.

I finally saw the value in my friend's question. As boulders are popping up now, I'm trying harder to remember the advice of my Guide:

"Keep your feet forward and your knees bent."

I can already see that I'm getting less frustrated, less angry and less hurt when I do run across boulders that are in my way. And, to my amazement, with my feet forward and my knees bent, it's sometimes as easy as stepping up and over them or pushing off and going around. Praise God!

10

GOING FOR WHAT'S
IN YOUR HEART

I've been challenged recently to go for what's in my heart. By that I mean searching for that which is deepest in my heart and going for it. I only have so many heartbeats in life, and I want to make each one count.

A few months ago, I was praying about several things I was considering doing, but for various reasons I wasn't sure if I *should* do them or if I *could* do them or how things might turn out if I *did* do them. I'm a thinker by nature, and I usually pray about, think about and analyze every decision, weighing the pros and cons fairly thoroughly before coming to a conclusion. While this trait is helpful at times—and has spared me from some disastrous results—it has also lead to some serious "analysis paralysis," whereby I've been unable to come to any conclusions at all.

So a few months ago, while writing in my
journal, I listed out the various decisions I was
trying to make. As I asked God about each of
these decisions, I felt like He was asking me:
"What's in your heart, Eric?"

The question was like a jolt to my system.

Really? I thought. *What's in my heart?*

The answers came instantly, and I wrote
down each one:

- *I'd like to…*
- *I'd like to…*
- *I'd like to…*
- *I'd like to…*
- *I'd like to…*

As I looked at each answer, I thought,
Yeah, I guess I really could do each of those things.
Some of them were risky, expensive and not
likely to pan out for various reasons, but none
of them were sinful or unbiblical. In fact,
some of them were very honoring to God and
to others. When I found out what was deepest
in my heart for each decision, the answers
were clear—much clearer than I realized before—and I was surprised at how quickly
those answers came.

After a little more time in prayer, I decided to go for what was in my heart in each of the situations and see where they led.

In one case, I wanted to take my family on what has become a many-year tradition of snow skiing for a day, and there was a particular day that stuck out in my mind when we should go. It would be the very last possible day of skiing, however, as we hadn't been able to go until that time. The ten-day weather forecast looked terrible though... hot, actually! I couldn't imagine there would be any snow left. But that date and the details seemed so clear to me that I felt we should go ahead and plan the trip. Even up until the day before our scheduled trip, the weather reports still looked like it would be impossible for us to ski the next day! While my head said, "No," my heart said, "Yes."

We went and there was plenty of snow! The day turned out to be amazingly beautiful! We had never had such a unique day of "spring skiing" like that before.

A beautiful day of spring skiing with my family.

In another decision, I wanted to send a gift and a blessing to someone who I felt had wronged me in the past. I didn't know how this person might take it, and I didn't want to bring up old wounds. Yet he was embarking on a new season in his life, and I wanted to offer my genuine blessing—and honest for-giveness—as he headed into his future. While my head said, "No," my heart said, "Yes." I sent the gift as a blessing, along with a letter explaining why I had sent it. He received it gladly and sent me a note of appreciation. While it may not have resolved everything related to our past hurts, it was a good start and good for my heart—and hopefully for his.

I'm still working on and waiting to see how some of the other decisions will turn out. But I can say that I've felt good about the decisions I've made. Even with the very real risks and costs involved, I feel like I've chosen a path which makes for a richer, more abundant life, no matter what.

As I thought about each of these decisions, I thought about some other decisions I've made in the past year when I went with what was in my heart—in spite of where my fears might have taken me.

I wanted to take my two youngest kids to Israel this past Easter, but was warned by the tour agency that the trip would be more expensive over Easter and the sites would be packed. As time went on, I still felt I should do it, but I was concerned that the issues raised by the tour agency were very real and very valid. The company even cancelled the trip at one point because of these issues, so I looked into going on my own. While I found some good rates and availability at various hotels and sites, I was still worried about the crowds.

A few days before I needed to make a final decision, I decided to call the tour agency again to see if they had reconsidered. Not only had they reconsidered, but they now had 35 people signed up to go—and the trip turned out to be less expensive than any other trip during the year! The tour company just hadn't gotten back to me to let me know.

So I signed up. The company wrote back and asked if I would be willing to be the spiritual leader for the group, doing daily devotionals at each of the historic sites and baptizing those who wanted to be baptized in the Jordan River. That was exactly what I was already planning to do with my own kids.

I said, "Yes," we went, and my kids and I —and our group of 38—were all abundantly blessed. Instead of clamoring crowds, we found ourselves first in line at many of the sites for a variety of reasons. While the tour company was right to bring up their concerns,

I was glad I kept going for that which was in my heart.

Touring Israel with our group over Easter.

One last story.

I met with a group a few months ago who, for the past several years, has sent our ministry some gracious donations every month. This group stepped up a few years ago to help out when things were extremely tight for our ministry even though our type of ministry was outside the scope of activities they would normally help to fund. I appreciated their help at the time, as it was a compassionate response to a genuine need. With their help and the help of others who stepped in at that time, our funding has since gotten much stronger. As this group was recently re-evaluating their annual giving, they let me know that since we were in a better position ourselves, they were going to cut back their support in the months ahead, phasing it out completely within a year. I told them I was very thankful for all the help they had given us, and we set up a meeting to talk about the details of their plan for my own budgeting purposes.

Before the meeting, however, I felt like God was asking me again, "What's in your heart, Eric?"

I was honest with God and said, "I'm very thankful for all the support they've given us to date, Father. It's really helped to get us through a time when things were very tight. But," I added, "if I were to be fully honest, I would hope that after all this time of partnering together, they would *double* what they're sending us each month to help us go further than ever before, rather than scaling back and eventually phasing out their support. I would even be happy if they could just send us $1 a month—if only for the sake of feeling like they were 'cheering us on' in our ministry."

When I met with the group to discuss the phase-out details, they asked at the end of our conversation how I felt about everything. "For the record," I said, "my 'official' answer is that I'm very thankful for all the help you've given us. It's really made a difference for our ministry over the past several years, and for that I'm truly thankful."

"And what's your 'unofficial' answer?" one of them asked. "That's the one we really want to hear."

"'Unofficially,'" I said, "I'm still very thankful for all you've done so far. But after all this time of partnering together, what I would really love is if you could double your monthly support—and keep supporting us for as long as you can."

They thanked me for my candor and said they would meet to talk and pray some more about it all. A few weeks later, I got a call from the group. Rather than cutting back their monthly donations and phasing out their giving, they had decided to continue helping with their monthly support (although not double as I had suggested, but more than I was expecting). And furthermore, they had no plans to phase out our support at all! Instead, they were going to now consider us one of their ongoing, regularly supported ministries. This one decision would impact us for years to come!

In a follow-up letter the group gave me with all of the details, I was struck by one phrase in particular. It said, "We are here to *cheer you on...*" I had never mentioned that phrase to them at all! But that's what I was wanting most. It felt like God Himself had given me the answer to that which was deepest on my heart!

Once again, I had taken a risk—in this case a risk of appearing ungrateful or hurting the feelings of people who had become dear friends over the years. But once again, I'm so glad I went for what was in my heart. And in so doing, not only have I been blessed, but thousands of others will benefit from this group's ongoing generosity.

Thank You, Lord, for giving me the courage to go for that which is deepest in my heart!

11

BEING
WHO I AM

I was having dinner with a friend when the conversation became awkward. We were talking about a subject we hadn't discussed in a long time, and we didn't know where each other stood.

I could tell I was holding back from saying what I wanted to say, and my friend could tell the same. To ease the tension, my friend said, "Eric, how about this: why don't you just be who you are, and I'll be who I am. Then we'll take it from there."

Whoosh! In an instant, all of the tension left my body.

Rather than worrying about how my words might be perceived, I felt the permission to just "be who I am"—in this case to speak freely—thereby advancing our conversation by leaps and bounds.

A few days later I was flying out west to meet with some people I had never met before. I was nervous about the meeting, and I was afraid I might feel "very small" in the presence of people who were rightly considered by many to be "very big."

As I was praying about the meeting, asking God to use our meeting to bear fruit for His kingdom in whatever way He wanted, I began worrying about what I should or shouldn't bring up during our meeting. In answer to my question, I felt like God said: "Be yourself, Eric. Be who you are. And I'll be who I AM!"

Whoosh! In an instant, all of the tension left my body.

Rather than worrying about how my words might be perceived, I felt I had permission to just "be who I am"—in this case to relax and enjoy this time of meeting new people— knowing that God would be who He IS: the great "I AM."

Over the next few days, as I met with person after person during the meeting, I was able to truly be myself and enjoy the moments as they came. I laid down any agenda I might have had and often just thought, *What would I do if I were to just be who I am?*

When I saw one of the "very big" people walking towards me carrying a stack of chairs to the meeting room, rather than thinking of what I should say or how I should say it, I thought, *What would I do if I were to just be who I am?* My answer: *I'd offer to help carry the chairs!*

I offered, he accepted, and I began making trips back and forth with him just carrying the chairs.

It was so simple! I knew I could trust that if God had something *more* for me to say or do, He would prompt me to do or say it. But in the absence of His prompting otherwise, it was easy to know what to do next: just be who I am! And in so doing, not only was I blessed, but so were those around me, even if it was in the most simple of ways.

This isn't to say that "being who I am" isn't without risk. There's always some risk in letting down our walls—and some walls are good and right for the protection of ourselves and of others. Even my friend warned me during our dinner conversation that dropping walls doesn't always end well. Life is messy. People are messy. But what a blessing to be able to share what was truly on my heart that night. And as my friend said later, "I know you, Eric, and I had to trust that no matter where our conversation went, something good would come of it."

I'm still experimenting. I'm still exploring. But I'm enjoying the process, asking not only what God wants me to do, or what Jesus would do—which are both terrific questions —but also "What would Eric do?" What would I do, given the way God has created me, gifted me and wired me? And then doing it, just being who I am and letting others be who they are—and letting God be who He is: the great "I AM."

12

TELLING
YOUR STORY

Last year, for the first time in my life, I decided to sit down and write out my full story—the story of how I came to put my faith in Christ and what's changed in my life since I took that momentous step.

I wrote the story under a pen name because, even though I had told the story many times, I had never shared all of the details in such a personal way. I wasn't sure if I would ever publish it at all, and I didn't want anyone to know it was me who had written it in case I decided against publishing it when I was done.

But by the time I got to the end, I knew that this was a story that *had* to be told—with all its ugly bits and happy bits and funny bits intact. I offered the book to several publishers, many of whom were initially interested, but none of whom would eventually publish it, saying it was too secular for the Christian market, and too Christian for the secular market.

So I published it myself. Within the first 24 hours, it went to #10 on Amazon's best seller list in the category where stories like mine are posted! Hallelujah! (I would still love for a publisher to pick up the book and take it to places I could never take it on my own. But in the mean time, I'll just keep sharing it with as many people as I can!)

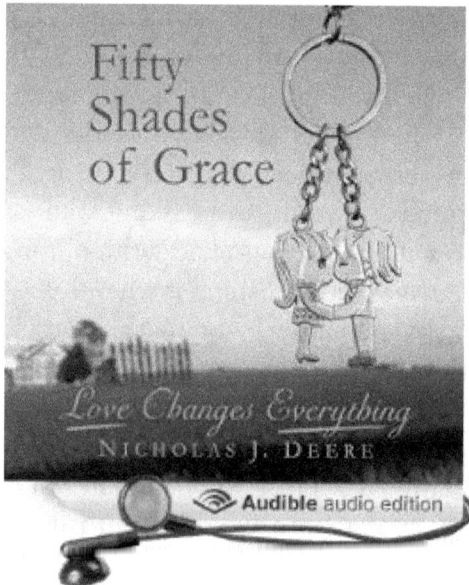

My story... now in paperback and audio!

After I began sharing my story in this way, other people said they were touched by it and asked if I could help them tell *their* stories about how God had worked in *their* lives. I said I'd be glad to help.

So this year, I've prayed about and committed to helping five other people tell their stories, two of whom have just finished their first drafts. And what incredible stories they are! It's amazing to see what comes out when people are given the freedom to tell their stories, holding nothing back, and seeing how interesting, unique and genuinely intriguing each story is. As a friend told me when I was writing my story:

> *"Every person has a million dollar book inside of them. They just have to tell their own story—but they have to be brutally honest when they tell it."*

I'm looking forward to sharing my friends' stories with you when they're finished. One is by a professional model who came to Christ and was able to deal with the ugliness she still felt inside. Another is by a woman whose husband went through a horrendous crisis in his health which sent my friend back to the foot of the cross daily. While the details of each of their stories are different, the theme is the same: God had walked with them every step of the way.

Such stories are endless. As the apostle John said after writing down his story:

"Jesus did many other things as well. If every one of them were written down, I suppose that even the whole world would not have room for the books that would be written" (John 21:25, NIV).

Maybe you've considered writing down your story. Maybe you've already started writing. Maybe you've wanted to tell your story, but you're afraid of what others might think about you if you do. But as author and pastor Rick Warren says,

"Every saint has a past, and every sinner has a future."

Can I encourage you today to tell your story? Write it down, pass it around and let others see what Christ has done in your life!

I, for one, am fascinated by stories of faith to see how God has worked in other people's lives. In fact, that's why I love reading the Bible so much. It's filled with stories of *real* people, who have lived *real* lives, and who have interacted with the *real and living God*.

I'm thankful that others have taken the time to write down their stories so I can learn from them. If you've been encouraged by hearing what God has done for others, think how others could be encouraged to hear what God has done for you.

What's your story? Maybe it's time to tell it. Will you pray with me?

Father, thank You for walking with us through the stories of our lives. Help us to be willing, eager and ready to tell our stories with others who desperately need to hear the words of hope that we can give them, hope that You will be there for them every step of the way as they live out their own stories. Use our words to touch people in a way that no one else could ever touch them. And as we share, may Your name be magnified, glorified and honored all along the way. In Jesus' name, Amen.

13

DROPPING TO
MY KNEES (PART 1)

This fall, I'm hoping to start a new series of messages on the topic of prayer and how you can have a more effective prayer life.

I've been working on this series for more than five years, but for various reasons, I have not yet felt it was ready to share with you. But the past few months, I have found myself dropping to my knees more often than ever, and I feel the time is right to share these messages with you now.

Recently, when I hear about something that's happening, or someone shares with me what's going on in his or her life, it often seems like the only appropriate response is to literally get down on my knees and start praying. As a side note, I'm not normally prone to just dropping down to my knees. I'll pray, yes, and I have prayed on my knees before. But what's new lately is that I feel compelled that there's nothing *better* I could do than to physically get down on my knees and pray— whether that means getting out of a chair, turning around and kneeling down, and putting my head and my hands down on the chair I was sitting on; or putting my head face-down in my pillow in the middle with my knees tucked up under me on my bed; or sometimes even dropping down to my knees as I'm going about my day, wherever I happen to be. In one way, I feel awkward doing this. But in another way, I often feel this is the only thing that seems right to do in the moment. As Abraham Lincoln has said:

"I have been driven many times to my knees by the overwhelming conviction that I had nowhere else to go."

There are so many things in life that require prayer, and no other response seems to compare.

Will you pray with me?

Father, thank You that we can come to You in prayer anytime, day or night, whether on our knees, on our chairs, on our beds, or walking throughout this magnificent world You've created for us. I pray that You would speak to our hearts today about how our prayer lives can be more effective and how we can have richer conversations with You. Speak to our hearts in a way that only You can do, guiding us in the best next steps we can take to grow in our faith, to grow in our devotion to You and to touch the lives of others through prayer. We ask this all in the strong name of Jesus. Amen.

14

DROPPING TO
MY KNEES (PART 2)

Last week I wrote to you about how I've been doing a lot of praying on my knees lately, something that I've done from time to time over the years, but not as often as in these past few months. After I wrote that message and sent it out, an interesting thing happened.

I was at church later that night for our Sunday evening worship service. I was on the worship team at our church that day and had already played the keyboard for the morning service. We have an identical service every Sunday evening, so I thought I knew the routine just fine. Our worship team was waiting backstage in the green room for our cue to go out and take our places to lead worship when the senior pastor, who was preaching on stage, decided to have a special time of prayer with the congregation before we came on stage. With all of the recent violence in the world, he felt we needed to pray in a special way. He didn't say anything other than to pray along with him.

I had just stood up along with the rest of the worship team, to get ready to go on stage. Then, without giving any other direction, our pastor simply knelt down on the stage and began to pray. When he dropped to his knees, I remembered my message from earlier that morning which I had entitled "Dropping To My Knees." I thought, *I should probably get down on my knees right now!* But I also thought, *But we're about to go on stage as soon as he's done praying; I'd better stand here and be ready.* Yet without another moment's hesitation, I was compelled, once again, to drop down to my knees. I did and immediately began praying.

Within seconds of my going down, I noticed that our whole worship team had done the same. There was no question on their parts either; no hesitation whatsoever. It was the only response that seemed right. I was floored, quite literally. We all prayed like that for several minutes, and when we were done, we simply stood up and walked onstage to lead worship. Our kneeling down to pray didn't interrupt the flow one bit. In fact, I'm sure it helped the flow tremendously.

Why am I so resistant sometimes to just drop down on my knees when it seems to be the most natural thing in the world *after* I've done it?

Later that night, I saw that the production assistant, who was giving us our cues back-stage, had snapped a picture of our prayer time. She posted it online, thankful to be part of a church and a worship team who were willing to get down on their knees and pray.

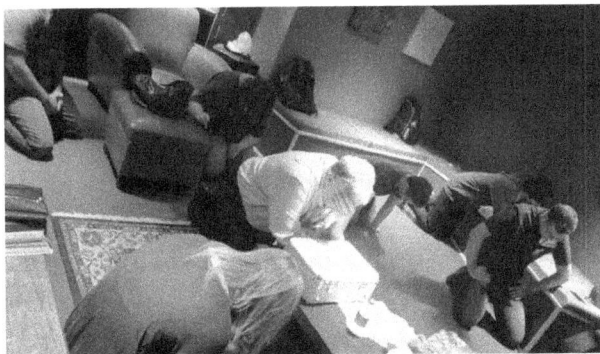

Our worship team spontaneously praying on our knees backstage.

I normally wouldn't post a picture like this, as it seems odd to do so. But like the production assistant, I too was so thankful for the same reasons. I felt there was no better response that we could make to our pastor's call to pray than to join him by praying on our knees.

Last night, I had another experience down on my knees. I was playing a game with my kids out in the back yard when the ball we were playing with bounced out into a field of soybeans that had grown up around our house. We could see the direction the ball went, but we couldn't find it when we walked out into the field as the beans had grown to be about two feet high. I said to my son, "If we could just lay down on the ground and look under the leaves at the base of the beans, I think we could see it. But," I added, "I really don't want to lay down on the ground." A moment later, guess where I was! Laid out flat on the ground!

Not seeing anything, I got back up onto my knees. And there, a few rows over, nestled at the base of the plants and hidden from view by the leaves above, was the ball. I was instantly transfixed, thinking,

Some things are simply seen better when we're down on our knees.

As it is with finding lost balls, so it is with prayer: some things are simply seen better when we're down on our knees.

Will you pray with me?

Father, thank You for letting us get down on our knees at any time (or in our hearts at least, even if it's not possible physically to get on our knees) and to come to You in prayer. Thank You that You hear our prayers and answer them, sometimes showing us things that we never would have seen had we not been on our knees. Thank You for others who model this kind of prayer for us, whether it's a pastor, a friend, or even Your Son, Jesus, as He prayed in the Garden of Gethsemane. Thank You for helping us to see on our knees that which we might never see any other way. In Jesus' name, Amen.

15

PULLING
WEEDS

I woke up early on Tuesday morning to do
something I really didn't want to do: pull
weeds. I don't usually mind pulling
weeds, but this was the last patch of what had
become a week-long project of pulling weeds,
and I was wearing out.

At first it was kind of fun. I was able to put
on some headphones, get down on my knees
and even take time to pray while I was down
there. But after a week of pulling weeds, I was
wearing out. I didn't know how much longer
it was going to take. I knew what I had to do
though—and that was to just keep pulling
weeds.

I decided not to worry about how long it
would take, but to just keep going forward
with the task at hand: pulling weeds. I got
down on my knees again and began to pull.
Surprisingly, after an hour of pulling, I was
done! And not only with that patch, but since

it was the last patch, I was done with the entire project that I had been working on for a week! The end had been right around the corner. I just didn't know it. All I knew was that I just had to keep pulling weeds.

Pulling weeds...going, going...and finally gone!

Yesterday morning, I woke up with another task at hand: recording a new song on the piano that I've been wanting to record for several months now. Unlike pulling weeds, this was a project I really *wanted* to do. But when I woke up yesterday morning, I felt like I was facing the same final patch of weeds again, and I had no idea when I would ever be able to finish the recording.

All I knew was that I just had to keep going and keep taking the next step that was right in front of me. Amazingly, within an hour, I had made huge strides in the recording process. By the end of the day, I had finished recording and editing all of the individual sound clips in order to turn them into one seamless and beautiful song.

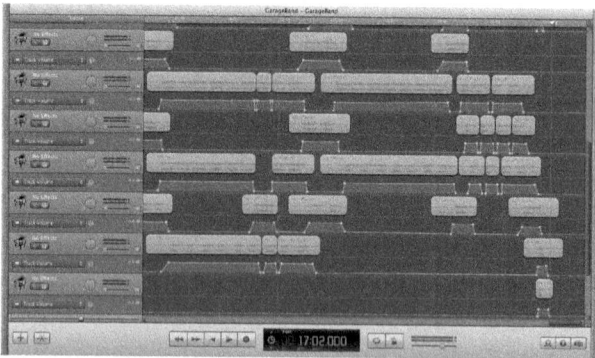

The final note (the purple square in the bottom right corner)

I still have a few more "next steps" to take

until the song is finished completely, so I can't share it with you yet. But here's a picture of the final note of the song in the bottom right corner of what has to be the longest and most complicated song I've ever recorded.

One last story.

I've been working through an unresolved situation with a friend for the past ten and a half months. While I believed there would be a resolution at some point, I felt like I had done everything I could do on my end, and I had no idea when that resolution might come.

This week I decided to take a personal prayer retreat for three days. While I'd been planning to do a prayer retreat with others at the end of the year, I thought it would be a good time to set aside the same amount of time on my own and enjoy my own personal time with God. Most of my kids were away at a music festival, so I had time to think and pray.

On my knees in prayer that first morning, I laid out the various things I was praying about in my life. Later that night, my friend called, and during our two-hour conversation, things were resolved. I told my friend that I had just started a three-day prayer retreat that morning. I said, "If only for this conversation, I am so glad I set aside this time to pray." And I still had two days of "retreating" to go!

I want to encourage you today that whatever seemingly insurmountable task may lay before you, whether it's pulling weeds or recording a song or reaching a resolution with a friend, keep focused on the task at hand. Do what God has called you to do. Take the next right steps He has called you to take. Then trust the outcome into His gracious and loving hands.

Will you pray with me?

Father, thank You for giving us work to do here on earth, whether it's pulling weeds, recording songs, or building friendships with others. Lord, I ask that You would help us to stay focused on the tasks before us, not getting overwhelmed by all the things that need to be done, but moving ahead with the next right thing we know to do. Lord, help us to accomplish all that You've put on our hearts to do—for Your sake, for our sake and for the sake of all those who will be touched by our efforts. In Jesus' name, Amen.

16

HOLDING
NOTHING BACK

Like many of my messages, this one is very personal. But I hope that giving you a peek inside my heart will be helpful. With that preface in mind, here's what I'd like to share.

About a year ago, I fell in love. It was quite unplanned and quite unexpected. I was talking with a dear friend from long ago and far away when all of a sudden, I was smitten. I don't know how it happened, but suddenly I was captivated—and I couldn't let it go.

I didn't tell anyone about it for two months, and I didn't tell her about it for three. I just kept it all close to my heart, talking to God, asking Him what He wanted me to do, and asking myself what I would want, if I could really choose to do whatever I wanted.

After three months of praying on my own, I felt like I should tell her. I sent her a note and asked if we could talk. She said, "Yes," she'd be glad to, and we picked a day to get together.

The night before we met, I asked God what He wanted me to tell her, and I felt like He said, "Let her know your heart, your fears, your prayers, your requests. She will be able to help you straighten them out." I would have loved to do that, but it seemed like that would be way too much to share, way too early, and way too risky.

But it also felt like this was what God really wanted me to do. I asked Him, "Is there any scripture to confirm this?"

I opened my Bible and began to read a conversation between Samuel and Eli, as recorded in the book of First Samuel, chapter 3. Samuel was hesitant to tell Eli something that God had spoken to his heart, but Eli told Samuel to tell him everything, word for word, holding nothing back. The next words seemed to jump off the page:

"So Samuel told him, word for word. He held back nothing" (1 Samuel 3:18, MSG).

Again, God spoke to my heart: "Hold back nothing, Eric. Hold back nothing. It's important for her to hear it and you to say it. Hold back nothing."

The next day we met, and, over a cup of hot chocolate, I shared with her everything that was on my heart—all that I had been praying about during the previous three months—holding nothing back.

In the months that followed, we talked and prayed, exchanged emails and texts. We never dated, never kissed, never held hands. In fact, I didn't even know if she had any feelings for me at all beyond our mutual friendship. All I knew was that God wanted me to share all that was on my heart, holding nothing back.

Six months later, I had finally finished sharing all that I could think of that was on my heart. I felt like I was a campfire that was being stoked with firewood continually until there was no more wood to throw on the fire. I had shared everything; there was nothing left to say; I had held nothing back. All I could do now was pray.

Not long after this, I was on tour in Israel and found myself standing on the Temple Mount, that hilltop in Jerusalem where Abraham once stood as he laid his son, Isaac, on the altar before God. I felt like God wanted me to do the same with this relationship. I had poured out my heart and said all I could say. Now He wanted me to lay it down before Him. So I did.

Months passed, and I heard no response. Then last week, I got a call. My friend had had time to process all that I had shared, and she was ready to respond.

As much as she felt honored by our friendship and appreciated all I had said, she felt that she wasn't the one I was really looking for—that she was a placeholder for the one who was to come. She was glad to be that placeholder, to prepare my heart for that person in the future, but she couldn't see herself as being that person.

I was disappointed, of course, but somehow I agreed with her! I knew that what she was saying was absolutely right. She really had helped me to straighten out all of my thoughts and feelings, fears and prayers. I was so glad I had shared with her all that I had shared. While I could have been tempted to see her response as a rejection (and if it was, it was the kindest rejection I had ever felt), God spoke to my heart to say that it wasn't a rejection; it was an acceptance—an acceptance of

God's will, His perfect will, His BEST will, for both of our lives. *God's will is always good-will,* even when it doesn't come in the form we might have expected.

As the ancient writer Epictetus said:

"I am content with what happens, for I know that whatever God chooses is better than what I choose."

I could have also been tempted to think that I had just wasted almost a year of energy —mental, physical and spiritual energy. But God stopped me in mid-thought and said,

"Time spent seeking My will with all your heart, soul, mind and strength is never wasted. It's always invested, and it will pay huge rewards for years to come."

It made me think of another quote, written by an unknown author, that says:

"Nothing lies beyond the reach of prayer except that which lies beyond the will of God."

I believe that is true with all of my heart. I

am thankful I sought God with all my heart, soul, mind and strength. I am thankful that I shared with my friend all that I shared, holding nothing back. And I am thankful for the answer which has come.

While I was hesitant to share this with you as it is so personal and so fresh, I know that the fruit often tastes sweetest when it's fresh off the tree. May we all enjoy it together.

Will you pray with me?

Father, thank You that we can come to you anytime in prayer, seeking Your perfect will with all our heart, soul, mind and strength. Thank You that our time in prayer is never wasted, but always invested, and that it will pay rewards for years to come. Thank You for friends who let us share with them freely, and thank you for their gracious responses. And Lord, thank You for the reminder that Your will is always goodwill. In Jesus' name, Amen.

17

DRAWING WATER FROM YOUR WELL

As a writer, I'm often pouring out to others that which has been poured into me. I'll hear something that intrigues me, I'll put it into practice in my own life, and then I'll share what I've learned so others can enjoy it, too. I used to think of this as if I were being handed a cup of cool water, taking a good, long drink, and then, if I liked it, passing that cup along so others could taste it for themselves.

But I've come to realize it's not as simple as just passing the cup along. It's more like having the water poured over me and letting it filter through the soil of my life into my own personal well. When I later draw out that water and give it to others, it has been filtered and flavored in a way that is uniquely mine. The water may come from the same Source, but it now has a unique flavor, a flavor that is unique to my own personal well.

I told a friend I wanted to send her something I had written which was based on something she had shared with me. Before I sent it, I said, "Of course, you've already heard this before, because you're the one who shared it with me!"

To which she replied, "Oh, no, I'd love to read it. I'm looking forward to seeing what the water filtered through your well tastes like."

I thought her statement was precious and profound, something which I've pondered and savored ever since. On my wall at home, I have a small wall hanging that a young man had given me after I visited his church in the Philippines. I had shared a personal message with him from my heart, and he was so touched by what I said that he went out and bought this wall hanging to let me know how much my words had encouraged him. It says:

"You are special. God sends each person into this world with a special message to deliver, with a special song to sing, with a special act of love to bestow. No one else can speak your message, or sing your song, or offer your act of love. God has entrusted these only to you."

A special wall hanging in my home given by a friend.

The young man who gave it to me had written on the back of the wall hanging, "Thank you for enlightening me, for leading me into the right path, and for letting God use you."

As I look back on what I shared with him in my message that day—now almost twenty years ago—I realize just how unique that message really was. It had been drawn from the well of my own personal encounters with God, and God had used it to touch him in a very personal way.

When you take the time to give out to others that which has come from your own personal encounters with God, you're giving people water that is uniquely from your well—a well which God has spent so much time developing.

That's one of the reasons why I love reading the Bible so much. I'm able to draw water from the wells of people like David and Abraham, Esther and Ruth, and especially Jesus. Each of them had a unique walk with God. Each of them received water from the same Source. Each of their stories and encounters with God has been filtered through his or her own unique soil. In turn, each of their stories adds to the richness and flavor of my own relationship with God.

You have your own unique well, too. God has poured water into you from His deep, deep well and filtered it through the soil of your life. Like Evian water that has been filtered through the soil in a small town in the

French Alps and is now shipped all over the world, the water in your well is costly and precious. Why not draw it out and share it with others? No one else can speak your message, or sing your song, or offer your act of love. God has entrusted these only to you.

18

EXCAVATING
MY HEART

When people ask me how I'm doing, I know they genuinely want to know—and I genuinely want to tell them. And overall, I'm doing good, really good. But I'm also not immune to something that I imagine many of you have experienced as well. Every once in a while, and especially in the last few months, I've found myself bumping into that thing called "loneliness."

It's not that I don't have friends or family. It's not that I don't enjoy a deep and personal relationship with God. It's just that sometimes, in the midst of walking out my life, I feel like I'm walking all alone.

I bumped into it again last week when a friend called with some heartbreaking news. As I tried to digest the words—and the possibility of facing yet another major loss   I realized I had not just bumped into loneliness; I was about to become engulfed by it.

I was walking through the grocery store when it happened, while I was picking out food for the week with my youngest daughter. Suddenly I felt like I couldn't take one more step. (I *could* have taken one more step. I just felt like I couldn't.) I mentally scanned through my list of friends I could call or text so at least someone would know what was happening in case I melted down into a puddle right there in the frozen food section of Walmart.

But then my daughter came back with another item on our list, so I just kept walking. I kept checking things off my list. And for the next half hour, I battled my inner thoughts and emotions, trying to just focus on the next item on my list, and the next, until I finally made it to the checkout lane. I knew that this feeling would pass if I could just keep taking one step at a time, as feelings like this have passed before. But I was so thankful when, later that night, I got home and was able to crash into my bed, letting sleep take over and do its restorative work in my heart and soul.

The next day I talked to a friend and shared what had happened to me. She, too, had bumped into this kind of loneliness and

had sometimes had been engulfed by it altogether. What she learned in that place, however, and what she shared with me, so touched
my heart that I wanted to share it with you.
She said:

> *"That loneliness is God's excavation of the
> ground, of a place in someone's heart, of a place
> that God is going to fill. But He's purposely not
> filling it yet. He's purposely leaving a space. And
> every time that feeling comes, He's taking a scoop
> —sometimes a bulldozer-sized scoop—but He's
> taking a scoop and making room in your heart."*

She continued:

> *"And God wouldn't do this if He wasn't intend-
> ing to fill it. When God's trying to take us deeper
> with Him, when He makes a space, He will fill it.
> He's intentionally not filling it because He's mak-
> ing the right place. And I think, based on the
> goodness of who He is—the utter goodness of who
> He is—there is no other answer. I don't think
> those are wasted moments. I think those are very
> real and very important moments."*

It makes me cry just to think about it—cry

with thankfulness for a good, good God who wastes nothing in our lives if we'll give it to Him.

Rather than feeling like life is trying to rip something out of me, I can now see clearly that God Himself is the One who is at work. God is doing a work in my heart, taking bigger and bigger scoops, in order to increase the capacity for whatever it is that He wants to pour into those newly opened spaces.

I'm thankful for a new vision of what's going on inside. I'm thankful for family and friends to whom I can reach out when I need someone else on the other end of the line. I'm thankful for a God who I KNOW is for me —and who I KNOW is for you—a God who really does want to work all things for our good.

The next time I feel that loneliness come upon me, I have something new to try. I'm hopeful that I'll be able to truly say,

"Father, thank You for taking another scoop. Thank You for digging deeper and deeper in my heart in order to take me deeper with You. Thank You for excavating my heart, for making space for more and for increasing my capacity to love You

and love others in a way that goes beyond anything I've ever experienced before. Thank You for always being FOR me and for holding those spaces open in my heart until the exact moment when You decide to fill them. Help me to not try to fill them with anything other than what You're creating them for, because I want more than anything to be filled with all that You have for me. I trust You, and I trust Your goodness in this situation, as I do in all things. In Jesus' name, Amen."

And the next time someone asks me how I'm doing, I can genuinely say once again, "Overall, I'm doing good, really good," because I know that God's got this, too.

19

RECALIBRATING
MY GOALS

Question: If you're stranded on a desert island, what 3 things would you most want to have? Answer: Michael Phelps, a saddle and a gold medal on a stick!

I've been watching the Olympics these past two weeks, and I'm inspired. I'm inspired to see what people can do when they put their minds to it, with Michael Phelps being example #1. He had a dream, he went for it, and he worked hard to attain it.

I've also been reviewing my own goals for this year—goals which I set back in January— and I'm inspired to pick up the pace to see what I can still accomplish by the end of the year. Unfortunately, I've fallen behind on some of my goals. I've stopped working actively on others. And I've found that the targets for one or two of my goals have moved.

But with the fall fast approaching, and the end of the year coming into view, I'm inspired to recalibrate my goals and keep pressing forward.

If you read my goal-setting message at the beginning of the year, you might remember that one of my goals was to write a complete script and score (the dialogue and music) for a new musical based on a book my wife and I had written a few years back about the real-life Saint Nicholas who lived in the 3rd and 4th centuries A.D.

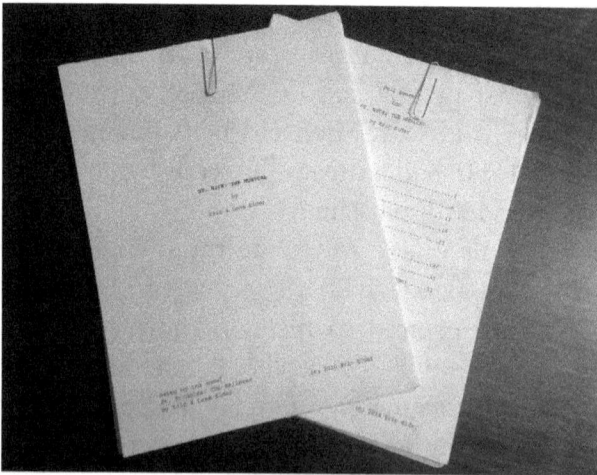

One-third of the finished script and score for St. Nick: The Musical.

I'm pleased to tell you I've finished writing a third of the script and a third of the score!

But I still have two-thirds's to go—and only a third of the year left to get there! So this week I had a decision to make. I could either get discouraged that I've fallen behind and give up on the project altogether, or I could pick up the pace, press on and keep moving forward toward my goal. As I looked at that goal again this week, remembering why I set it, how I thought I could accomplish it and the progress I've made to date, I'm ready to dive back into writing again.

I had another goal this year to lose some weight. By the middle of the year I had lost half of the weight I had hoped to lose for the year, and I was right on target. But over the past six weeks, I've taken a break from tracking and losing weight, only to find I've gained some of it back. So this week I had another decision to make. I could either get discouraged that I've not only stopped making progress toward that goal, but have actually started going backward, or I could pick up the pace, press on and keep moving forward toward my goal. And as I looked at *that* goal again this week, remembering why I set it, how I thought I could accomplish it and the progress I've made so far, I'm ready to dive back into tracking and losing more weight, too.

It wasn't easy to decide to jump back into these goals, but I had a small victory this week that gave me a boost.

I was mowing a large patch of grass behind our house with a push mower—not an electric push mower, but a "reel"-type hand push mower like my grandpa used to use. The grass had gotten taller, so pushing the mower through the grass wasn't easy. I kept having to stop and clear out the grass and sticks that kept the reel from spinning (and honestly I was thankful for the break each time so I could stop, catch my breath and wipe the sweat from my face). I didn't think I could finish the whole patch, and I was tempted several times to give up and go inside.

But as I was pushing the mower through the grass, I started thinking about all of my goals for the year—why I had set them, what I hoped to accomplish by doing them and what might happen if I actually achieved them —and I was inspired to keep going with them all… and with the mowing, too! Even though I was ready to give up after 20 minutes, then 30 minutes, then 40 minutes, I kept pushing on until 45 minutes later, I was done! (And yes, this is the same patch of grass where I was pulling weeds a few weeks ago and had to give myself continual pep talks to finish that project, too!)

Fresh off this victory, I went back inside, took a shower, then pulled out all of my goals again for the year. Yes, I had fallen behind on some of them. Yes, I had gone backwards on others. And yes, I was going to have to take aim in a different direction to hit the rest. But I knew—like every Olympian who competed in Brazil these past two weeks—that if I kept on track and kept putting in the hard work it takes to achieve my goals, then I would certainly achieve more than I could ever achieve otherwise.

And somewhere along the way, I just might win a gold.

20

GOING DEEPER

Since the beginning of the year, I've shared nineteen messages with you on a variety of topics, from goal-setting and goal-keeping to keeping your feet forward and your knees bent so you don't get sideswiped by the boulders in your life. Today I'd like to share one more message with you in this series, a message I believe will help each of us go deeper in our walks with God than we've ever gone before.

Before I started this series, I was telling a friend that there were some aspects of my walk with God where I felt like I had hit bedrock. I felt like I had dug as deep as I could, and there was no further I could go. If I tried digging any further, my shovel would just clank against the rock, over and over again.

I wasn't frustrated by this feeling, however.

In fact, I was quite comfortable to rest right where I was!

But my friend told me about a character in a movie who was running through a desert when, all of a sudden, the ground beneath him started to give way. A huge hole opened up, revealing a rushing river below. As the ground gave way, the character jumped into the newly opened hole and into the rushing river underground, taking him further and deeper than he had ever gone before.

My friend saw me as that character in the movie, and couldn't help but believe that there was a rushing river beneath my feet as well that God wanted me to jump into.

I was intrigued by the idea, but I didn't know what to do about it. The ground beneath me was seemingly impenetrable. What else could I do?

But one of the things I've also been trying to do this year is trying to grow in my own personal relationship with God. For the past few months especially, I've been trying to deliberately focus on what *my* unique relationship with Him looks like, not superimposing onto it what other people's relationships with Him look like.

Knowing that this was on my heart, and combining it with the vision of the idea of the ground giving way beneath my feet, my friend encouraged me to do something I had never done before. It sounded almost heretical, at least to someone like me who loves the Bible and has read it many, many times. My friend asked me to consider setting aside the Bible for a period of time in order to focus very intentionally on my own personal relationship with Him.

I thought the idea was too risky. Unnecessary. I didn't want to do it.

But while I was in Israel earlier this year, walking down a road where Jesus likely walked, I read these words in my Bible, words spoken by Jesus Himself to the religious leaders of His day—leaders who had studied the Scriptures for years, inside and out. Jesus said:

> *"You have your heads in your Bibles constantly because you think you'll find eternal life there. But you miss the forest for the trees. These Scriptures are all about Me! And here I am, standing right before you, and you aren't willing to receive from Me the life you say you want" (John 5:39-40, MSG).*

I was struck to the heart and challenged anew. What *would* it look like if I were to fast for a period of time from relying on other people's relationships with God as a substitute for my own, even if those others included people like David and Moses and Paul. What would—and does—*my* unique relationship with God look like?

I decided to give it a try for a time, praying and asking God to build my relationship with Him even stronger than before. And just last week, I finally broke through!

During our worship service at church, our pastor was talking about prayer. Everything he said was speaking directly to my heart. It was as if God Himself were prefacing every sentence with my name.: "Eric, …" "Eric, …" "Eric, …" I jotted down notes as fast as I could, knowing that God was using these words to speak to me directly, encouraging me to take the next step towards going deeper with Him.

When the message was done, we sang a song to God in response to all we had just heard. As I sang, I felt like I could practically see the ground beneath my feet starting to give way! I could see a hole opening up right there in the concrete floor! And as the ground was giving way and the floor was falling out, I could see it clearly: that rushing river that I couldn't see before!

When the song ended, the shaking stopped, and the concrete floor was perfectly solid once more—hard as rock. But I had seen the river, and I very much wanted to jump through that hole and into the river, letting it take me further and deeper than I had ever gone before.

The next few days, I was captivated by that image of the river beneath me. I felt like I could almost slip down through the ground at any moment and into the water below. But then I'd stop myself. I wondered, *Do I really want to do this?* I was tethered, in a good way I felt, to all of these other people's relationships with God—and I wanted to *stay* tethered to them. What would happen if I were to really unhook and explore what my relationship with God was like on my own?

On Wednesday, I found my answer!

I was listening to a speaker at a men's breakfast at our church, when suddenly the speaker shouted: "STAY TETHERED TO JESUS!" I knew that instant exactly what God wanted me to do! All I had to do was to release my tether from relying on the experiences of others, and tether myself to Jesus Himself, which is the very thing I would love to do as well! I love the Bible; it's my favorite book in the world. But I don't want to miss the forest for the trees. I don't want to be holding onto the words about Jesus so tightly that I miss taking hold of Jesus Himself!

Yes, Lord! I thought. *That's what I want!*

I took the other end of my tether, and I hooked it firmly to Jesus. I looked into the hole below me that had now opened up again, and I knew I could make the jump whenever I was ready. And I was ready, knowing that Jesus was holding tightly to the other end of my rope.

I jumped!

What I hadn't expected was that at the very same moment that I jumped, Jesus jumped, too! AHHHHH!!! Now I was in a total freefall, with no ground beneath me and no rope above me. I looked over at Jesus, shocked that He had just jumped over the edge at the same time that I did! He just looked at me and smiled as we continued to hurtle down toward the river below.

That wasn't what I had expected. It was better! I was doing this with Jesus. Praise God!

Over the past few days, I've been heading down that river with Jesus, going further and deeper than I've ever gone before. But that's not the end of the story.

Yesterday morning, I woke up thinking about this new journey. And while I love the idea of having Jesus with me, I kept saying over and over, "I don't want to go alone." (He's a good friend; He knew what I meant.)

Then I looked up above us, and in the same way I had seen Jesus and me jumping over the edge of the hole and into the river, I now saw one or two dozen more people at the edge, parachuting over it! They were coming along with us!

They were coming with us, but I felt like God was saying that they weren't ready yet to get in the river with us. They wanted to watch as we went along. But one by one, God was saying, when they saw the joy that it brought us to be in the river, they *would* join us in the river, too. And not just one or two dozen, but hundreds and thousands—and eventually hundreds of thousands!

I wouldn't be alone! We'd all be rushing down the river together, going further and deeper than we'd ever gone before.

How about you? Want to come along? I'd love to have you join me!

Just make sure to "STAY TETHERED TO JESUS!" (And don't be surprised if He jumps when you do!)

I'm convinced this isn't the end of this story. The best is yet to come!

ABOUT THE AUTHOR

Described by *USA Today* as "a new breed of evangelist," Eric Elder is an author, composer and creator of *The Ranch*, a faith-boosting website at WWW.THERANCH.ORG.

Also by Eric Elder:
Two Weeks With God
What God Says About Sex
Exodus: Lessons In Freedom
Jesus: Lessons In Love
Acts: Lessons In Faith
Nehemiah: Lessons In Rebuilding
Ephesians: Lessons In Grace
Israel: Lessons From The Holy Land
Israel For Kids: Lessons From The Holy Land
The Top 20 Passages In The Bible
Romans: Lessons In Renewing Your Mind
St. Nicholas: The Believer
Making The Most Of The Darkness
15 Tips For A Stronger Marriage
and *Fifty Shades Of Grace (under the pen name Nicholas Deere)*

To order anytime, please visit:
WWW. INSPIRINGBOOKS.COM